TRANSFORMING UNCOMMON GROUND

THE GARDENS OF VLADIMIR SITTA

TRANSFORMING
UNCOMMON
GROUND

THE GARDENS OF
VLADIMIR SITTA

Tempe Macgowan

Foreword Catherin Bull
Prologue Julian Raxworthy

Frances Lincoln Limited
4 Torriano Mews
Torriano Avenue
London NW5 2RZ
www.franceslincoln.com

Transforming Uncommon Ground: The Gardens of Vladimir Sitta
Copyright © Tempe Macgowan 2009
Photography copyright © Anthony Charlesworth, Walter Glover,
Rod Parry, Vladimir Sitta
First published in Australia in 2009 by Bloomings Books Pty Ltd
First Frances Lincoln edition 2010

Saffron House, 6-10 Kirby Street, London EC1N 8TS.
A catalogue record for this book is available from the British Library.

ISBN 978-0-7112-3128-3

Printed and bound in China
1 2 3 4 5 6 7 8 9

CONTENTS

Communist Party Retreat, Czechoslovakia, 1976

While surprises come in many guises, it is unusual for them to come in the form of a garden. Although gardens are places of the imagination, they are by definition usually places of retreat and relaxation rather than of active intellectual engagement. That is what makes Vladimir Sitta's gardens so special and this publication so valuable. This book showcases the surprising private gardens Sitta has designed and tells us something of their creation.

Those of us who are challenged to explore what the idea of garden and landscape means in contemporary times will find this volume a basic reference. Vladimir Sitta provided the work, sketches, design, photographs and notes about the making of these gardens; landscape architect and design writer Tempe Macgowan scripted the text; Bloomings Books, its editor and designer prepared the material for publication. They and the owners of the gardens themselves must be acknowledged and thanked for making these otherwise inaccessible private places available for readers.

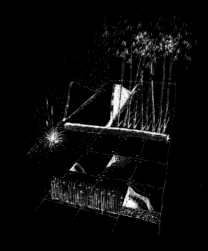

Sitta's garden design work challenges us in many ways, contradicting established norms. It is at once poetic and technologically creative — and in both, fearlessly so. While undeniably special, his gardens are also places of everyday life — full of children, dogs, clothes lines, living. They reveal the elemental forces of nature, earth, fire, water and gravity which usually remain invisible to urban dwellers. Through his artistry and the sensory, intellectual and imaginative responses that such artistry demands, we rediscover what such forces mean. Big experiences are packed into small spaces and every square metre of garden is exploited to the full for its poetic, sensory and functional potential. He teaches — and we learn a new formal language in the process.

The earth splits and heaves, revealing the forces that shape it. Water is a pool, but it

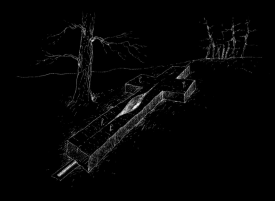

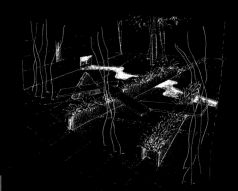

is also a harbour, a stream, a mist. It oozes, drips, laps, spouts and plays, begging us to experience its many ways of being.

In all this, Sitta's work confirms for us the importance and power of the garden as a laboratory in which to experiment and explore the ever-evolving relationship between nature, culture and our place in both. His work also demonstrates the importance of continually exploring that relationship and learning about it afresh.

The publication of this book has been made possible not only through the energy and dedication of its author, editor and publisher, but also with the generous assistance of that committed garden maker Dame Elisabeth Murdoch AO. Through continuing experiments in her own garden laboratory at Cruden Farm near Melbourne and her life-long interest in ideas about the evolution of the Australian landscape, Dame Elisabeth has contributed to how Australians think and feel about nature and their place in it. Like Sitta, she continues a lively engagement with the issues that gardens raise, supporting research and publications about landscape in all its guises through the Ellis Stones Fund (named for that other dedicated and original garden maker) in the landscape architecture program at the University of Melbourne. *Transforming Uncommon Ground: The Gardens of Vladimir Sitta* is a valuable addition to that growing collection of publications.

Catherin Bull AM FAILA
Elisabeth Murdoch Professor of Landscape
Architecture,
University of Melbourne
May 2009

Photographs of Vladimir Sitta's residential garden projects suggest his body of work is consistent, employing the formal design strategies and common landscaping materials of conventional landscaping. However, if we hold Sitta's drawings up against that same work, and imagine his strong personality cynically overlooking the whole scene, then his work is very different from the good taste it appears to embody.

Vladimir Sitta's design work is contradictory, juxtaposing opposites, or at the very least creating awkward adjacencies: pagan–Christian; public–private; subject–object; culture–nature; natural–artificial; specific–general; theoretical–practical. In reality these elements are not in opposition but in dialogue, with the emphasis on the difficult parts of the conversation. The most interesting aspects of Sitta's work also provide the strongest basis for discussion and critique.

To engage in such discussion is to look beyond what I refer to as 'Garden Porn' (carefully composed photographs of lush gardens) and examine personal aspects of Sitta's work. The most readily available means to do that, without delving too far into his biography, is through his drawings.

Drawing Therapy

Well before I knew anything of Sitta's work, it was a drawing of his that alerted me to his existence. That drawing, coupled with the fact that everything was not as it appeared in Australian landscape architecture, sparked my interest. I had seen his odd drawing on the last page of an edition of *Landscape Australia*, the professional magazine of the Australian Institute of Landscape Architects. Heavily drawn in black and white was a spiral staircase leaving a building, but spiralling back upwards to return to the building. A figure was climbing

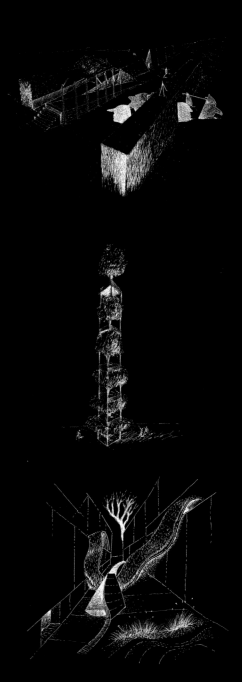

the staircase but at the top, where the stairs would logically re-enter the building, the person was faced with a hopeless blank wall — a strange drawing for a magazine that otherwise was seemingly obsessed with the bush.

Later, seeing Sitta's name again, I tracked down a biography that noted he was a recent émigré from Czechoslovakia, also the home of Franz Kafka. In the context of Kafka's *The Castle*, which describes a man's insane bureaucratic journey to enter a castle that seems constantly out of reach, the drawing of the staircase began to make sense. It embodied a certain type of experience, an experience of striving and frustration. That frustration with Australian landscape architecture still characterises Sitta, but is something you would not detect in reviewing his work.

Vladimir Sitta has collaborated widely with landscape architect Richard Weller under the moniker of Room 4.1.3, an enigmatic title that actually refers to a banal office at the University of Western Australia. Their most notable collaboration produced the Garden of Australian Dreams at the National Museum of Australia in Canberra. The sometimes difficult bond between Sitta and Weller was solidified by a common interest in drawing. On Weller's graduation from the University of New South Wales in the late 1980s, he asked his lecturers Helen Armstrong and Craig Burton where he should work. Weller's nascent work was as much about drawing and art as it was about landscape architecture, so his lecturers were pessimistic, reflecting that in Australian landscape architecture at that time 'design' was a dirty word. They suggested that Weller work overseas. However, in the interim they referred him to a strange designer from eastern Europe by the name of Vladimir Sitta who produced drawings similar to Weller's, and who was working for a Sydney practice detailing furniture in Sydney's eastern suburbs.

For his first meeting with Sitta, Weller was instructed to bring his drawings. Sitta pulled out his drawings too, and the pair sat at Sitta's desk and enjoyed an impromptu 'show and tell'. Their drawings spoke of a world of significance for landscape architecture beyond any practice, one that reflected the complexity of the cultural landscape well beyond the conventions of bins, seats and paving, which comprised much of landscape architecture practice. Frankly, there were greater things at stake: 'the experience of dwelling on the earth as mortals', as philosopher Martin Heidegger might describe it.

When viewed as an evolving set, Vladimir Sitta's drawings, or 'doodles' as he calls them, describe a world with some continuity, but one that is different from the world we see around us. To read the drawings is to see evidence of the alien world of Sitta's imagination, a virtual world. Many of Sitta's drawings focus on the

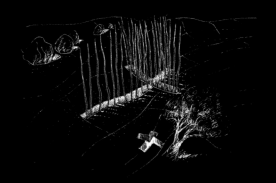

clear definition of strange objects placed in the centre of the picture, but at the drawings' edges, in the peripheral vision, there exists enough evidence of a context for the object to describe a physical (or metaphysical) milieu. Perhaps we need to occupy Sitta's drawings or nightmares in order to interpret them, to scope out the laws of his world. To do so, we will need to look more closely at his drawings. But it seems like a scary place, so let's not linger too long.

The landscape of Sitta's drawings is generally a sparse environment where the ground and the sky are the major elements. On a surface that is slightly curved or distorted through exaggerated perspective, the focus is usually on a singular element which may be an architectural object or the manipulation of a landform. The objects generally comprise combinations of natural and artificial elements, like trees or elevated platforms of

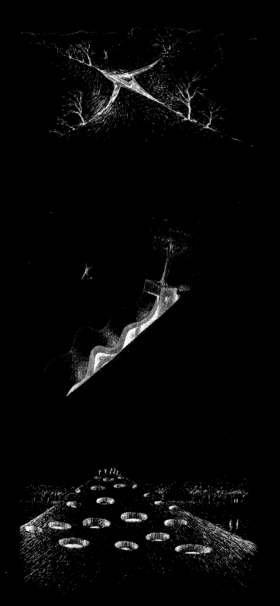

trees or similar, where the objects are cyborgs: fused natural and artificial hybrids that allude to a use, or misuse, of the natural. Few trees, birds and people occupy this landscape; when they do, they feel like the only living things in a dead landscape, like the lone child in his own small world in *The Little Prince* by Antoine de Saint–Exupéry. Sitta's drawings are black and white, a feature that lends a sense of pathos or the Gothic.

Much could be made of Sitta's drawings by Jungian psychoanalysis since many of them feature religious content, the cross being a common element, treated in many different ways. Sitta is not a Christian and sees the cross as a powerful and common symbol in many cultures. So, for him, the cross is a gestalt, a clear logical figure of wholeness. In his drawings the cross is given numerous renditions and many crosses are misused or misplaced. In some drawings the edges of the

cross are frayed into crumbling turf, like a rockface with fissures. The cross drawings are edgy, defiling a known symbol by changing its context in such a way that they reflect back on its usual sacred interpretation.

Other symbolic images appear in Sitta's drawings and signify a vision that also encompasses time. Crows fly in the sky or sit in trees, distant figures walk around the site. Time in this world is slow, significant and about duration: the time taken to invoke a spell, with the sense that something is imminent. This is not time as conveyed by banal landscaping — for Sitta, all time is heavy and pregnant with unfolding meaning. This aspect of his drawn world is evident in the assumption that you (a viewer) are watching the scene unfold. All his drawings use a two-point perspective which Sitta repeats with great prowess as a freehand artist. Objects in the space tend to come from the left, growing larger as they move into the view frame. This perspective is about controlling the view, about controlling interpretation, even as that interpretation is vague or enigmatic.

The format of a drawing is important because drawing is an activity, a process conducted in time where the minutiae of the steps in the process inform the end-product. Sitta's drawings are not about craft. Generally his drawings are on A4 bond paper, the kind of paper used in a printer or photocopier. Drawn in black ink, they are stored in plastic-sleeved presentation binders. The drawings are not stored in a grandiose folio like artworks but filed as professional working documents. This is not surprising when one considers that landscape architects produce drawings for a living. However, these drawings are not strictly professional, and few of Sitta's drawings are of gardens per se. Consequently there is a

content as personal expressionistic creations and their mode of production and storage as objective office documents. This disjunction between the personal and the professional characterises much of the interest of Sitta's work.

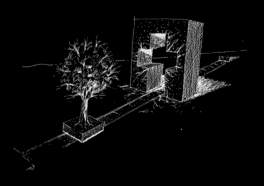

The drawings are not produced for a specific project but are site-less in terms of the 'real' world, dwelling instead in Sitta's macabre universe. Faced with a new project, Sitta flicks through his binders and chooses an appropriate drawing. So each site becomes an opportunity to test a distinct concept, a concept separate from site or client. The site then represents a real place to deploy what was a virtual idea. Sitta smiles and agrees when I suggest that the drawings may be cheap therapy. The translation of 'Drawing Therapy' to 'Garden Porn' is an interesting and occasionally disappointing process.

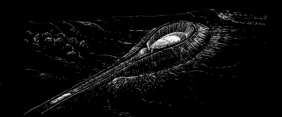

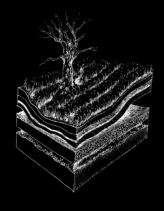

Garden Porn

While Sitta does not always have the opportunity to build his symbols (particularly his crosses, which have never been built as far as I know), the Red Garden gives the clearest translation of his drawn language into a landscape. Like the Japanese garden, the Red Garden is designed to be seen in a composed view. Tilted red plates of stone emerge from a red landscape with a pool of water below. The shape of the plates angled down to the sides and into the peripheral vision directly mimics the two-point perspective of Sitta's drawings. The angle of the stone plates effectively forms the line work that some artists might use to guide the rendition of a perspective drawing. The foreground of the red perspective sculpture is a useable surface, a landscaping element, but really the landscape is a three-dimensional picture.

As well as cultural symbols like the cross, much of Sitta's work revolves around cultural interpretations of natural elements, particularly trees which are given torturous treatment (one wonders what trees have done to him!). In both drawings and built projects Sitta removes trees from the ground and leaves them to die, to become sculptures, the complex growth geometries of roots and limbs revealed as form not organism. Sometimes trees are turned upside down, their roots becoming their branches. In his Chaumont sur Loire exhibit, Sitta created a wall that arced and tapered, through which trees protruded with the roots on the outside and the limbs inside. This is an idea he also developed on other projects. It is not only trees that receive such symbolic treatment. The ground also has a symbolic presence for Sitta, with objects being set in, buried in or lifted from it — the ground is the benchmark.

Many of Sitta's garden spaces feature focal elements, with the rest of the space simply providing a context. This object-based approach, more architectural than landscape, could be characterised as being more about the field in which objects sit than about the objects themselves. A common motif in Sitta's work, again featured in his drawings, involves strips or slashes through a neutral but high quality ground. These slashes often run along a rough line dissecting the garden plan, though rarely symmetrically, exemplifying the now-common Japanese compositional system of asymmetrical balance. In these slashes Sitta has added a three-dimensional element with plants like bamboo, or used fire or water at ground level. The slash works only because of the openness of the field, which tends to be composed of one material, such as pebbles or gravel, or possibly sheets of black water. The success of such strategies is not a matter of plan organisation but rather of detail realisation. The simple figure relies on

the disappearance of construction detail, so that the construction does not thicken the edge where the element joins the surface but keeps it fine, or makes it disappear completely. To keep a garden clear like this, to keep the material pristine and consistent is actually a functional exercise because circulation and use, as well as banal issues like drainage, must be dealt with first to predict impacts on the garden forms.

As a designer, and more importantly a builder of gardens, Sitta has long been ahead of international trends in garden design. His work, especially that of his company Terragram, has been heavily published in glossy garden source books, often as the only Australian contributor. That Sitta produces glossy gardens seemingly made for photography — my 'Garden Porn' description — rather than public spaces that question the relationship between culture and nature,

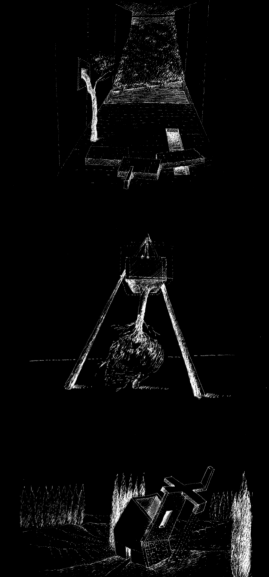

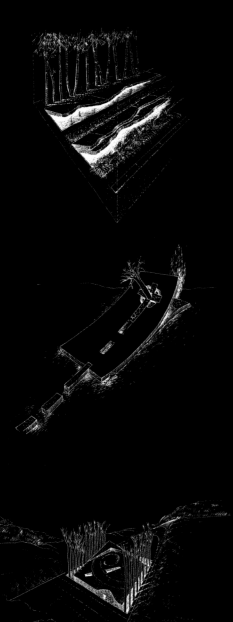

seems a cruel joke that is not lost on Sitta. Garden work for the wealthy middle class has formed the majority of his work. That is because he is good at it, and the reason why many architects choose to work only with him, despite being 'a grumpy old bastard' by his own admission.

While commercial and media gardens have propounded the 'outdoor room', 'a Japanese feel for your garden', the use of decorative mulches and such, Sitta created such elements ten years beforehand to little or no Australian acclaim. Much of this work uses the outdoor space as a building setting or for 'lifestyle', a tendency that has now relegated much design to the selection of finishes or the use of material as symbols of good taste. This type of work draws heavily on the formal and material strategies of Modernist architects like Richard Neutra, who 'blurred the line between the inside and the outside'. Architectural historians have traced the lineage of this design approach from Modernist architects who travelled to and studied trends in Japan, like Bruno Taut, Walter Gropius and Frank Lloyd Wright. Rather than utilising these qualities and strategies as simply parts of a bourgeois palette, Sitta's work seems more self-conscious and deliberately opulent in a way that renders the spaces as works of spatial sculpture, rather than as gardens, though the material and setting are 'gardenerly', as are the rationale and client brief. Even so, Sitta acknowledges cynically that much of his work is 'outdoor decoration'.

While the refinement of materiality and detail has made this type of garden a more spatial and experiential affair, with much talk of Zen, some aspects of what might once have been termed 'a garden' have disappeared. In these gardens the plant material is used for 'form', a single species can form a monoculture of massed planting, as 'living sculpture' or for low maintenance. In the process of plants having this role, and of the garden being tightly controlled as a context or as a sculpture, the opportunity for clients to customise their gardens and to undertake gardening is lost or at least downplayed. The intersection between garden design as an art and gardening as a craft is an area in which the modern garden often misses the opportunity to involve clients in the meaningful development of their own gardens.

It is interesting and endlessly frustrating to Sitta that he has primarily undertaken residential garden designs in Australia because, as a landscape architect, his passionate interest is the design of public space. His main built public project in Australia is the Garden of Australian Dreams, developed with Richard Weller. However, overseas, both separately and together, he and Weller have won countless competitions for public spaces. Few of these competition

designs have been built, but all feature some of the symbolic content that regularly features in Sitta's drawings, together with rational and conservative urban design strategies. Sitta can be scathing about working for public authorities in Australia, which he characterises as being devoid of strong personalities who will foster innovative projects, lamenting that there is no 'public Medici', no patron. These comments reflect a belief that design is a subjective not objective affair and designers, with their individual visions, should be supported by their clients.

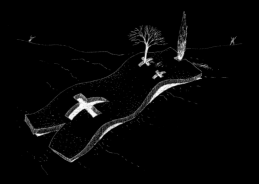

Sitta's rationality in urban design reflects what could seem a contradiction in his work: extreme pragmatism. In all of Sitta's built work and also his critique of work by his peers (which can be scathing; for example, describing a colleague's work as 'a urinal with a view'), Sitta expects perfection in the realisation of the design. This intense interest in landscape

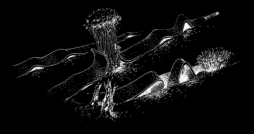

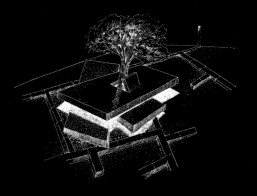

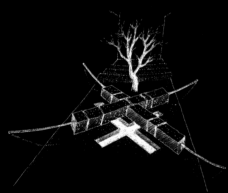

detailing partly explains his popularity with architects who are often shocked by the poor detailing abilities of landscape architects. The irony of Sitta's own propositions in drawings being fanciful and often physically impossible, while at the same time being obsessed with realisation, is yet another of the contradictions in his design work.

Australia is a country of immigrants and Sitta is yet another 'wog', as he calls himself, even if his provenance is different from the norm. While Australians are obsessed with the sense of homeliness in this landscape, Sitta's work in drawings and gardens builds places around the notion of placelessness and suggests that even when at home we occupy an 'uncanny' or 'unhomely' zone which does not allow us to be complacent about our location but keeps us aware of our occupation of a landscape and the experience of being here, anywhere.

Julian Raxworthy

Senior Lecturer, School of Design

Queensland University of Technology

June 2009

HARBOUR POOLS

19

SKY POOL GARDEN

Water is often viewed simply for its utilitarian functions, with its aesthetic qualities discounted. So it can take quite a leap of the imagination to find different conceptual ways to express its complexity. For instance, how many forms can water take and how can it be contained? It can be a harbour, rain, a stream, a single drop, a dreamy mist or an expansive view.

Water is the essence of this garden. With a swimming pool and the harbour at the far end of this steep site, the garden is structured with several garden rooms allowing ease of access around the residence, while also presenting an exploration of water in a range of dimensions.

On entry to the property, a visitor passes through a neat front garden where a pathway leading from the front gate is defined by a water sculpture, reminiscent of a design by Italian architect Carlo Scarpa. Near the front door, a narrow channel of water cascades into a reflecting pool. The flow continues as the main courtyard of the house opens out to a vista of the harbour and the swimming pool. In this final form, 'water flows over the cantilevered glass edge into a hidden spillway, effecting a fluid surface that bleeds into its aqueous background ... with a wet edge adjoining the surrounding pavement, and forms both a mirror sculpture to the sky and an unexpressed place of recreation' (Sitta's project notes).

Location Sydney, Australia

Narrow channel of flowing water with carved headstone, glass cascade and fibre-optic lighting
Previous page: View of swimming pool and harbour

Clockwise from top left: Hand-carved stone birdbath; Door to courtyard and floating stairs; View of front garden

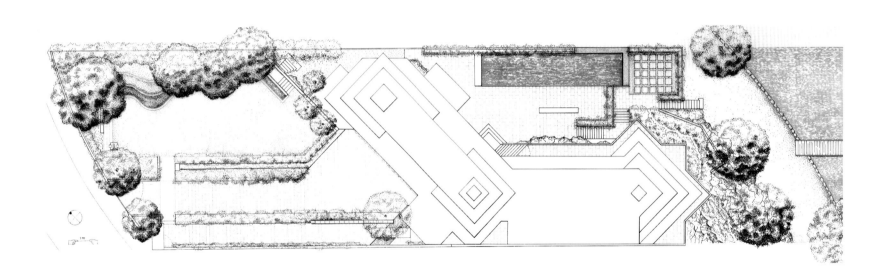

Sketches and plan of garden

Views of cantilevered swimming pool with wet edge and courtyard

LINKING THE HORIZON

O n a largely inaccessible site, Sitta has contrived a water view and access to Sydney's magnificent harbour for his clients by splitting and splicing walls, and inserting an outdoor entertainment room. More than just an open outdoor space, an undulating timber deck nestled among outcrops of rock walls mimics the water's movement washing over the shoreline. The deck rolls into a spa pool suspended over the sand.

Location *Sydney, Australia*

Project Team *Vladimir Sitta, Robert Faber*

Timeframe *2005*

Architect *Luigi Rosselli Architects*

Landscape Contractor *Brooks Enterprises*

Contrasting textures and forms of the shoreline sandstone are evident here, from sections

of rough sea wall, to dressed retaining walls, niches and ledges. With all the quirkiness and

haphazard nature of Sydney, a door originally intended to be neatly inserted into a wall

now forms a distinctive feature that is more in character with its setting than the original

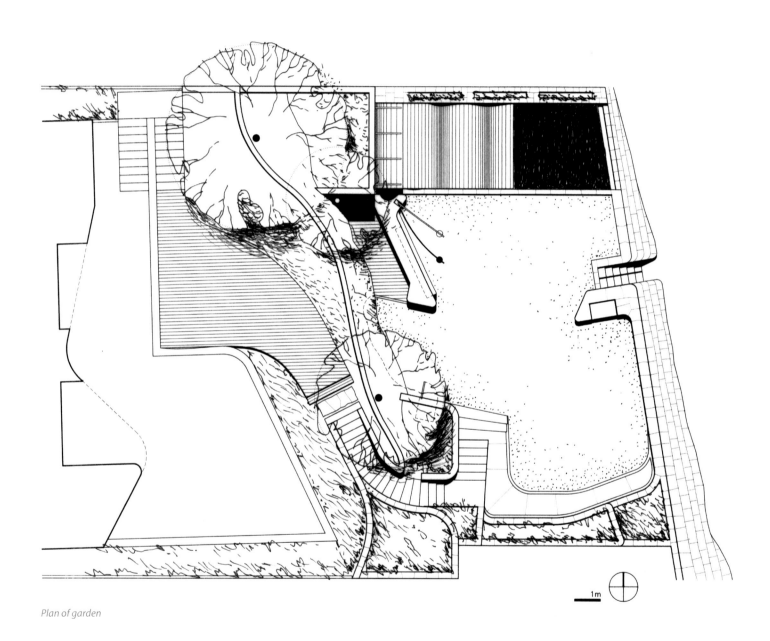

Plan of garden

1m

Above: Carved sandstone steps to the water's edge;
Detail of shower

The rolling deck

GARDEN OF REFLECTIONS

From the cliff edge of this garden, there is a visible sameness about many of the neighbouring harbour foreshore properties – they are concerned only with the view and display an irreverence to the site. This modernist house and garden provide an exception. The external spaces are designed for experiencing rather than viewing the harbour. They are filled with light and water despite the fact that leftover spaces around the perimeter and a front area provided the only places for a lawn area and a swimming pool.

Location *Sydney, Australia*
Project Team *Vladimir Sitta, Maren Parry*
Timeframe *1998–2000*
Architect *Allen Jack+Cottier Architects*
Landscape Contractor *Above the Earth*

From left: Chiselled blades of granite retain a planting area on the roof of the garage; Slabs of laminated glass reflect fairytale lighting
Opposite page: A glass spillway and water basin at the main entrance; The water mirror in the sculpture court
Previous page: View into entrance courtyard and limestone bridge

Creating flow and continuity with these fragmented spaces presented a challenge. Using the architectural elements of the house, Sitta found room to add still and running water, pockets of planting, light and shade, and reflections. These elements provide the continuity and ephemeral dimensions of a garden during both day and night, when 'dozens of laminated fibre optic lights … create a fairytale atmosphere,' Sitta explains.

Decent-sized courtyards provide play areas for the children. One grassed courtyard includes an enticing elliptical cave, colourful mosaics and a restful timber deck offering a perfect venue for sleeping out. At the harbour's edge, the peerless elegance of the swimming pool along the top of a low cliff greets the visitor. The pool invites swimmers to glance through the glass edge out to the harbour beyond. The design of this garden addresses every detail and opportunity, including a walkway to the rocks and caves below, encouraging a journey of discovery along the foreshore, to explore the rock pools for oysters and sea anemones or simply to revel in the harbour environment enjoyed by Sydneysiders.

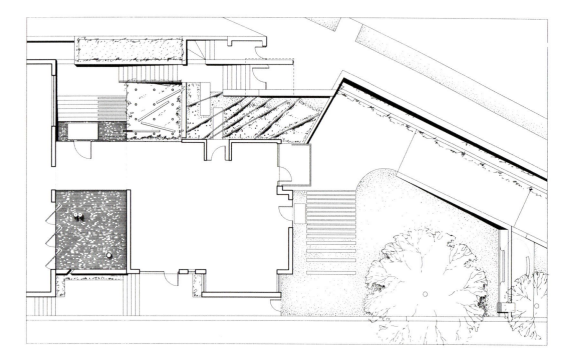

From left: Plan of garden; View of front garden with red 'grotto'
Opposite page: View of pool cantilevered over harbour shoreline; Detail of pools

WATERMARQUE

Overlooking a quiet inlet just a ferry ride away from the city, a tsunami of decks washes over the roof of this apartment block. The view of the inlet can be enjoyed discreetly from this rooftop. The rhythm of planting, a spa pool and over-scaled seats are ingeniously fitted into a relatively small space. The layout looks as though each of the elements has been cut into strips and layered on the rooftop.

Location *Sydney, Australia*

Project Team *Vladimir Sitta, Robert Faber, Anthony Charlesworth, Linda Halustok*

Timeframe *2007– 2008*

Architect *Allen Jack+Cottier Architects*

Landscape Contractor *Rowlands Landscapes*

Metalsmith *Belzebu*

Watermarque

2e Mosman Street

View of apartments from street
Previous page: View of penthouse roof garden

The rooftop apartment with decking, spa pool and planting. A copper chimney was incorporated to disguise a ventilation shaft

Within the building in a serene corner, a water feature provides a quiet source of pleasure and reflection and brings inside the essence and proximity of the harbour.

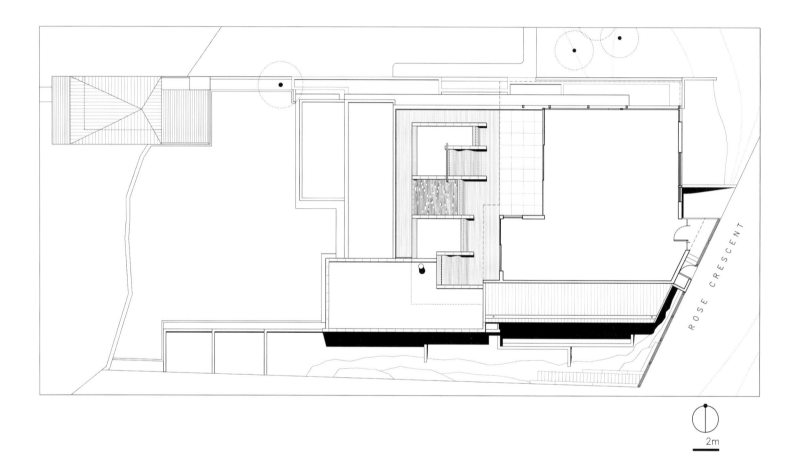

ROSE CRESCENT

2m

Plan of garden

Clockwise from top left: Interior water element in foyer space; View from penthouse apartment; Detail of glass water spout and spa pool

COURTYARD GARDENS

ODE TO WATER

The narrow strip of sand of an almost private, yet public, beach foreshadows little of the journey that begins beyond the house above. The former house and garden were completely overhauled, retaining only a stone wall and the swimming pool at the water's edge. This garden epitomises another ode to water where the visitor explores its presence from the front gate to the harbour's edge in its various poetic dimensions and transformations.

Water welcomes you the moment you open the front door and it continues to accompany your passage through the various levels of the house. A mechanised tidal pool where an island floats in a sea of water can be transformed into a stage for a piano recital or simply serve as a courtyard for an outdoor table. Cascading water leads to a quiet pool, a spillway and finally to the swimming pool and the harbour. Subtle detail in the pool – a stone blade with the Greek word for time, legible only when reflected in the water – adds interest and intrigue.

Location *Sydney, Australia*

Project Team *Vladimir Sitta, Robert Faber, Anthony Charlesworth, Linda Halustok*

Timeframe *2005–2007*

Architect *Alex Popov Associates*

Landscape Contractor *Rowlands Landscapes*

Pool Contractor *Neil Beecroft Constructions*

Metalsmith *Hi-Tech Precision Engineering*

From left: A granite blade inset with inverse writing on the water's edge; View of entrance forecourt from street level
Opposite page: The entrance forecourt with submerged brass grate, platform, water basin and black bamboo
Previous page: View of mechanised tidal pool when submerged

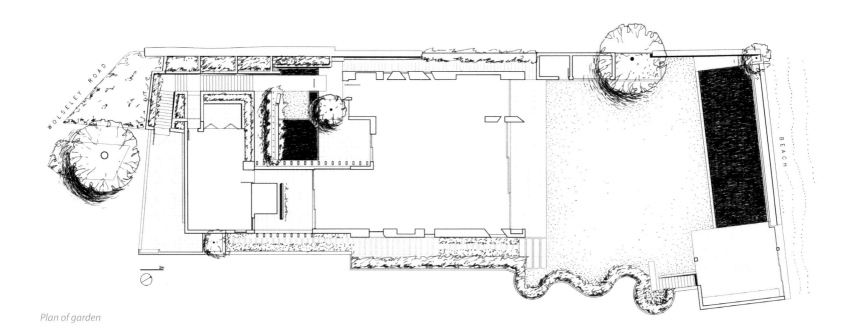

Plan of garden

The vertical wall of succulents; Harbourfront swimming pool with infinity edge

51

NECKLACE OF GARDEN ROOMS

Your home is said to be your castle and this residence is very much grounded in its location. Formerly an apartment block occupied most of this block. Even with this modern building of two apartments, there is still little room for a backyard, so Sitta designed some 'fragments rather than a garden'. With its hillside location, the building provides street access to both apartments, and Sitta's 'fragments' include an upper penthouse courtyard, swimming pool and terrace. His design notes describe these external areas as 'tranquil thresholds from a busy life; a prelude to a quiet, private life'.

One of these areas takes the form of a water garden that's semi-flooded and has an arrangement of fountains, spillways, pools and runnels, green moss walls, stepping stones and islands. Here the resident is passionate about animals and has statues of them throughout the house and even by the front door. Recently a 'pet' crocodile has come to reside here although it looks more like a living sculpture. In another courtyard, Sitta's 'prelude' takes the form of an 'interrupted journey' where you can perch on the edge of a golden yellow disc with a threshold of flowers at your feet.

Location *Sydney, Australia*
Project Team *Vladimir Sitta, Robert Faber, Anthony Charlesworth*
Timeframe *2006–2008*
Architect *Allen Jack+Cottier Architects*
Landscape Contractor *Rowlands Landscapes*

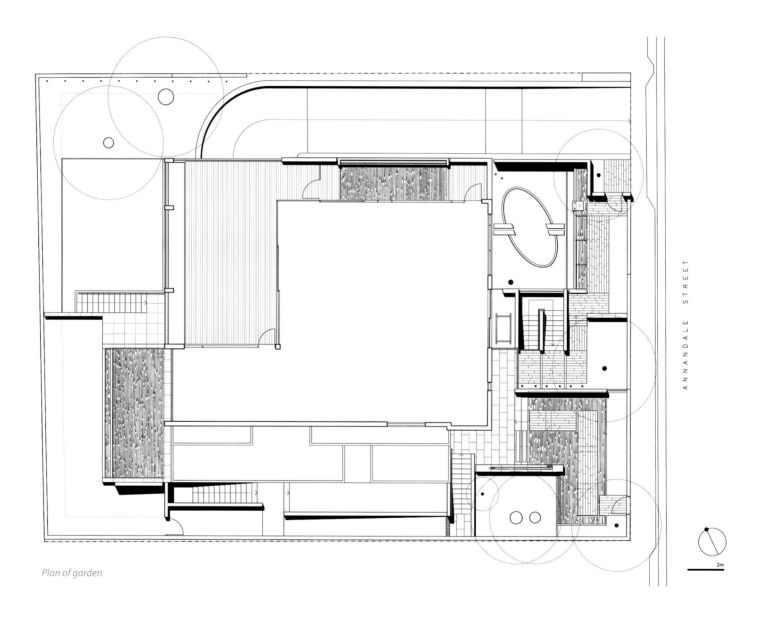

Plan of garden

ANNANDALE STREET

2m

From left: Lower apartment swimming pool; Penthouse swimming pool with cascading water spillway

BAMBOO COURT

The spatial limitations of outdoor private space present a common dilemma with the increasing densification of Sydney. It's a bonus when the residence adjoins a park and can borrow from its tree canopy. The design of this townhouse courtyard does exactly that. Compositional tricks create spatial illusions in the courtyard and the sense of a large outdoor room. Initially, with ample greenery in the park next door, overplanting in this courtyard was reduced, by thinning out bamboo to increase transparency and reveal more of the existing walls; some darker foliage was added to increase the perception of depth.

Location *Sydney, Australia*

Project Team *Vladimir Sitta*

Timeframe *1993*

Architect *Reg Smith*

Landscape Contractor *Client*

58

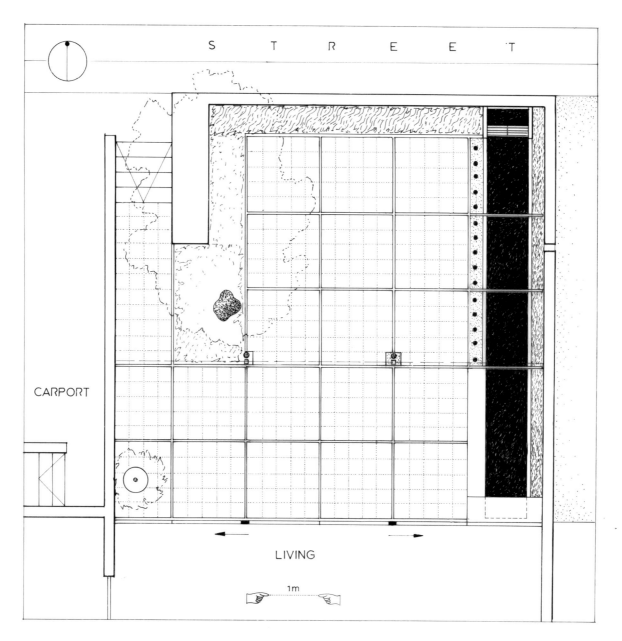

STREET

CARPORT

LIVING

1m

The plan shows how a grid can make a small space appear much larger

With a grid of travertine strips overlaying a narrow reflecting pool on one side of the courtyard, the sense of space is stretched horizontally and blends in at the edges. A cascade fills the courtyard with the soothing sound of falling water. With sliding doors opened from the residence, the living room nearly doubles in size and overlooks a space that now has a shifting focus and changing moods.

From left: The reflective pool at nighttime; The grid flows through to the boundaries in the form of travertine strips

BAMBOO GARDEN

Well-designed gardens provide a retreat – an escape to another world. Even in a small courtyard garden, it's possible to create this dream, and everything about this garden near Balmoral Beach in Sydney prolongs the journey between house and street and creates an enchanted space.

The 'journey' starts at a wall that is higher than those adjoining it and then continues along an elevated, smooth, axial granite path. The pathway passes through a forest of black bamboo (*Phyllostachys nigra*) which fills the view in the same way as many Japanese gardens with planting right under the windows of the house.

Location *Sydney, Australia*
Project Team *Vladimir Sitta*
Timeframe *1992*
Architect *Allen Jack+Cottier Architects*
Landscape Contractor *Bob Browning*

Embedded within the bamboo forest is a fountain where water quietly flows over polished black granite strips into a surrounding trough. The geometric stripes of the granite provide a striking contrast to the bamboo and water. Together they create the further illusion of light, reflection and mystery in an otherwise confined space.

Once in the garden you're immersed in a world of dappled light
Previous page: The elevated pathway leading to the entrance to the house

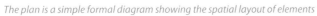

HOUSE

STREET

1m

The plan is a simple formal diagram showing the spatial layout of elements

BAMBOO GARDEN

THEATRE OF LIGHTS

In this compact parkside retreat, the distractions of the city are far removed and one's senses are alert to the pulse of nature's seasonal and daily rhythms. The garden nestles under the canopy of an adjacent park, immersing it in tranquillity. This space is also an entertainment area and a venue for the client's interest in Japonaiserie and the arts. An installation at one end of the garden captures the contemplative mood of a Japanese garden, while the remainder is left open for an unobstructed view into the park. The installation was developed as a series of layers using very few elements — a terrace, table, granite slabs, water and lights.

Location *Sydney, Australia*
Project Team *Vladimir Sitta*
Timeframe *1993–1994*
Architect *George Freedman Associates*
Landscape Contractor *Above the Earth*

67

Even in such a small space there is more to be revealed, including a threshold slab of rough granite, in which the natural fissures have been artfully enlarged to create a sculpture with engaging qualities. The fissures divide the slab into four sections, reflecting the four stages of life from birth to death, which Sitta refers to as 'The Journey'.

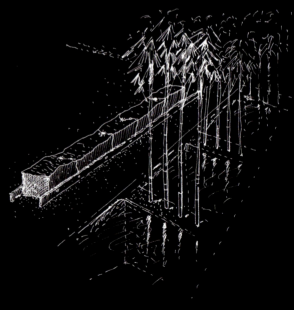

Even during the day the mist can dematerialise the elements in the garden; Sketch of the rough granite strips

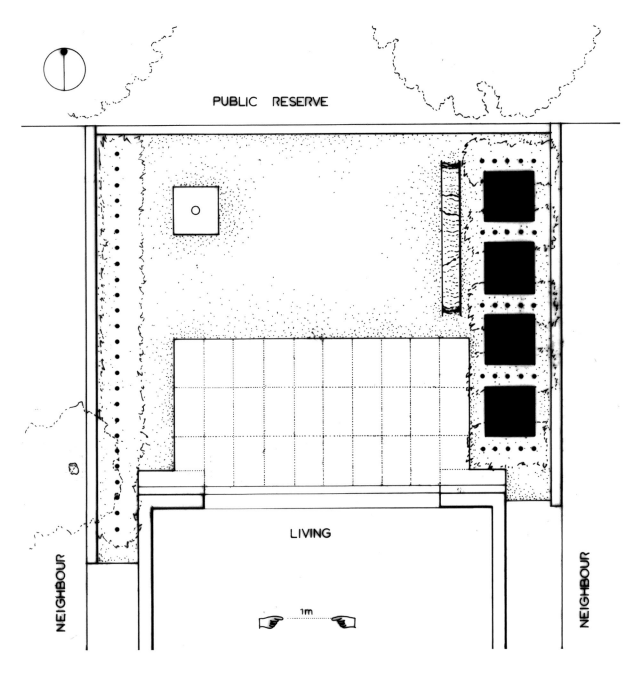

PUBLIC RESERVE

NEIGHBOUR

LIVING

NEIGHBOUR

1m

Plan of the space shows how deceptively small it is

THEATRE OF LIGHTS

WALKING ON WATER

This forecourt offers one of those poetic, dream-like moments that occur mysteriously and fleetingly — its ambience can be appreciated only by being in it. In a small space, the clients were granted the opportunity to walk on water. This intriguing element is created with a scrim of water covering a brass walkway which is either submerged or 'reveals a safe passage home', as Sitta explains. This all-too-real illusion is achieved with a mere flick of a switch. The forecourt even has different moods during night and day. During daytime, the water becomes a mirror reflecting the sky, walls and surrounding bamboo; while at night, shimmering lights transform it into a fairytale place.

Location *Sydney, Australia*

Project Team *Vladimir Sitta, Maren Parry*

Timeframe *1997–1998*

Architect *Allen Jack+Cottier Architects*

Landscape Contractor *Above the Earth*

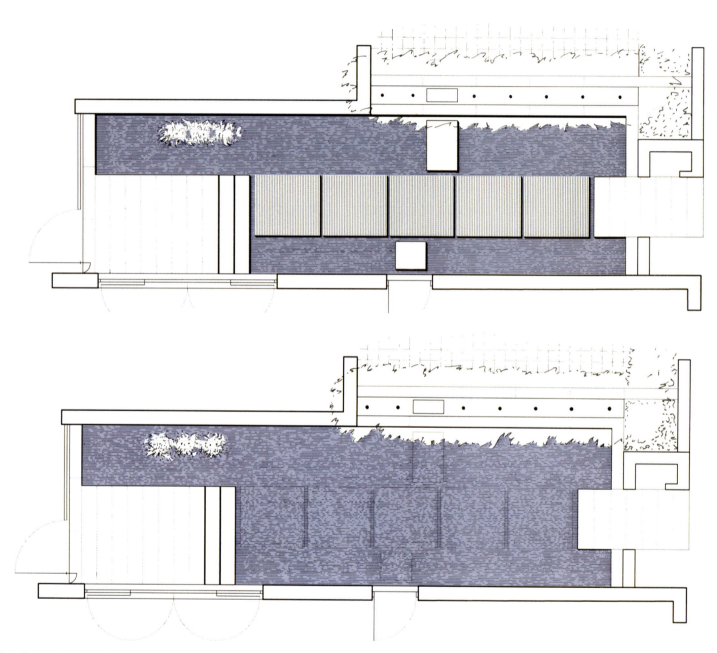

Plans showing the spatial effect of having the walkway submerged or not

Previous page: Walking on water

First page: The forecourt can be a dark mirror at night with the welcoming beacon of the entrance door

The different moods of the forecourt

T his courtyard has massive sandstone walls with the intimidating thickness of an Aztec temple. The harbour suburbs of Sydney are largely built on, or out of, such sandstone. In so many of its gardens, Sydney's notorious clay soils and poor drainage can often dictate their design — and this was the case here. This site was small and awkwardly shaped with some remnant ugly brick walls. The clients wanted to reduce its overall claustrophobia and create a contemplative place away from the surrounding dense urban environment. As with many such small spaces, the approach was to reconfigure it, to create new experiences and enlarge the sense of space.

Stonemason Carl Valerius, an Australian 'Zorba the Greek', extracting the garden from rock

After the excavating, exposing and shaping of a space outside the kitchen, a new courtyard emerged. The space now features a body of water, bamboo planting around the edges, a glass spillway set at eye level with the kitchen, and a striking 'Blue Rock' resting on a glass cube. The Blue Rock is an essential counterpoint to the muted sandstone colours that could have dominated such a confined area.

As can often happen on older sites, an unexpected, unused pipe was found during construction. This one left a scar on removal. The positioning of a sandstone block now conceals the scar by masquerading as a mystery door. With the juxtaposition and contrasting colour of the rocks, extricated from their natural context, this garden is now much more than the rock that shapes it.

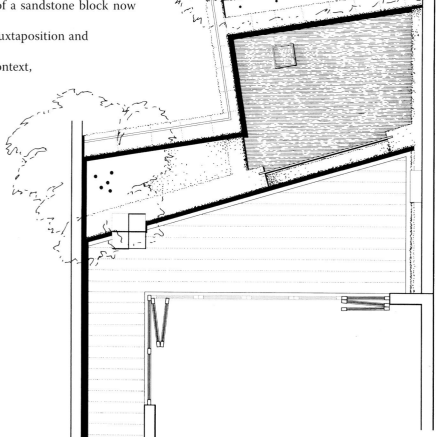

Plan of the awkwardly shaped site and its new layout

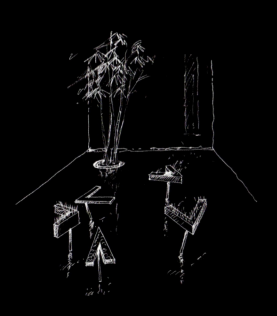

Clockwise from top left: Sitta often uses a Japanese arrangement of steps in small spaces; Water flowing over the glass spillway;
The Blue Rock appears to be a sailing boat in a large inland sea; Sketches of the courtyard

SURGEON'S GARDEN

The central void at the core of the house is a revelation, and reflects the trust, curiosity and patience of the client. When the architect, Keith Cottier, created this court from hollowing out the building, he took the opportunity to provide a seamless extension between interior and exterior space.

Location *Canberra, Australia*
Project Team *Vladimir Sitta*
Timeframe *1995*
Architect *Allen Jack+Cottier Architects*
Landscape Contractor *Above the Earth*

Above and previous page: The simplest of materials are used in the central core

This space inspired the following poetic description: 'fade into gravel, begging to be uncovered; at night, a small copper boat burns as an "eternal flame" filling the space with flickering light; a multi-layered scar suggests past sedimentation and upheaval, but now the space is nothing but calm, healed and completely harmless' (Sitta's project notes).

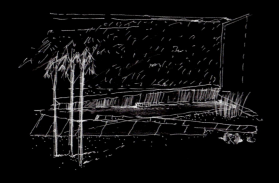

Clockwise from top left: Floating flame — a small vessel with a flame floating on the water's surface; Poetic text partially covered by gravel, inviting visitors to marvel at its meaning; Sketch of the garden

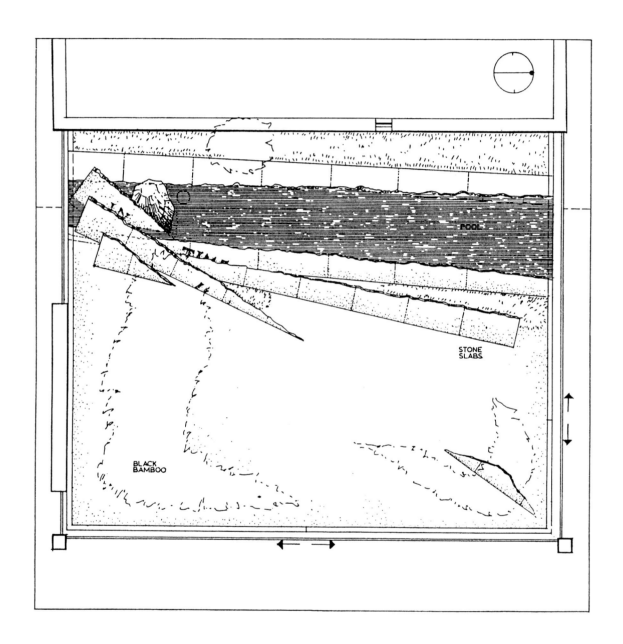

Plan of garden

The courtyard at night

SURGEON'S GARDEN

PLAYING IN WAVES

Where can you ride a wave, play and set up a fishing rod at the same time? In this small courtyard where space is minimal, the illusion of all three has been achieved with no water in sight. The wave is a slightly undulating timber deck which also serves as an oversized seat and play area. The installation of yellow fishing rods is a spatial device for plants to grow on which takes up no space; the rods are simply flexible, tapering sticks (minus hooks) which moderate the severity of a neighbour's wall. These are uplit at night, giving the impression of being on the water.

Location *Sydney, Australia*

Project Team *Vladimir Sitta, Robert Faber*

Timeframe *2002*

Architect *Chris Elliott Architects*

Landscape Contractor *Bates Landscape Services*

88

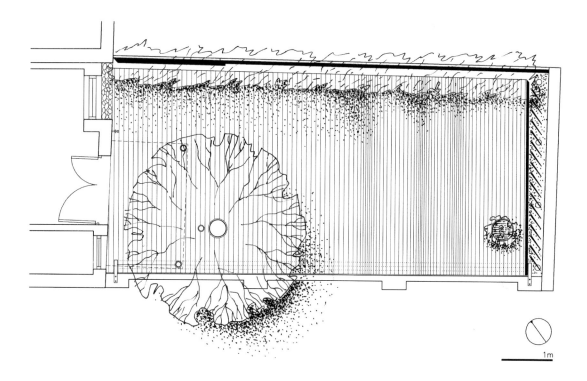

Plan of courtyard

Previous pages: The deck can be used in numerous ways – as a picnic area, for sunbaking or just relaxing

View of deck and fishing rods from above

FILMMAKER'S GARDEN

This tiny house is tucked away in a tight little corner of one of the densest areas of Sydney. Entering this confined space, visitors are immediately immersed in dripping greenery, creating the impression of an urban rainforest. Initially concealed from view is a wall formed from a vertical canvas of plants. In such a crowded area, space for a garden is limited, so every surface becomes one that's ripe for planting – even a vertical surface. This garden was conceived as a living laboratory to explore the idea of vertical green walls for an urban environment, a subject being researched by Frenchman Patric Blanc.

1998

2001

2003

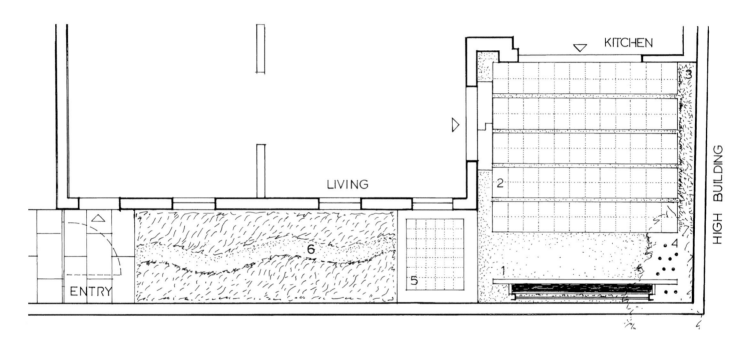

Above: Plan showing how simple it is to achieve so much in such a small urban space
Previous page: An urban rainforest

From left: Placing the plants in the fabric; The plants in the early stages of growth

Making the canvas wall was a complex process and one that the client could opt to retain or not. It is a soil-less planting process where the fabric is covered in pockets, in which small ferns are planted. At the top a pipe disperses water and nutrients and, with time, the plants take root in the fabric. While the canvas has endured various trials of water deprivation and the like, it continues to evolve. The local Sydney filmmaker who owns the house may not initially have appreciated the outcome of such experimentation, but she has an adventurous spirit and shows off her 'living laboratory' with relish to interested visitors.

Further reading: Ian Perlman, 'Uncommon Ground – Enclosed Spaces of Water and Walls: Projects of Vladimir Sitta/Terragram', *Via Arquitectura*, March 2001.

ART DECO

Typically the demarcation between public and private is well defined and the two domains are kept separate. In this case though, there is no obvious indication that the property entrance is a private area as it adjoins a public footpath and roadway – there is no vertical barrier to prevent trespassing.

An enclosing rhythm of hedges provides a prelude to this renovated apartment block's entrance. Capturing the essence of Art Deco design in its angular forms, the building also presents a sense of Italian modernism with its wall treatment. The hedges and planting though are where the richness of the design lies – the subtle layering and contrasting of colour and texture form an interesting collage when viewed from above.

Location *Sydney, Australia*

The entrance and forecourt are an extension of each other

The rhythm of hedges forms a sculptural painting

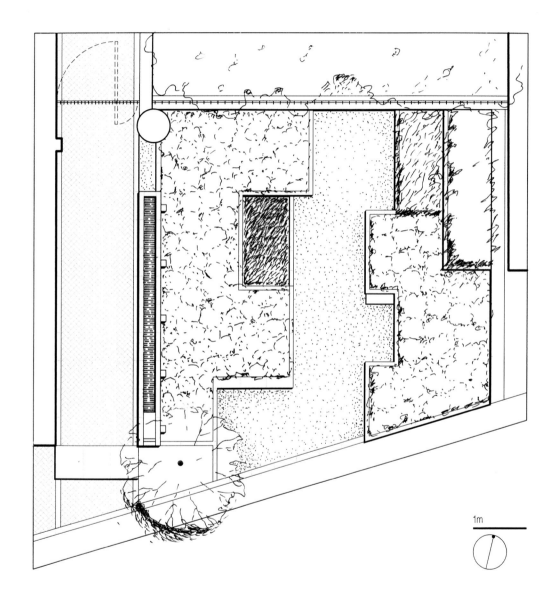

Plan of forecourt

T R E S P A S S I N G   I N T O   A R T   D E C O

SWIMMING POOLS

GARDEN OF GHOSTS

The idea of a private zoo in Sydney is beguiling, almost incredible, yet that is what this garden was in the 1930s. There's a tangible sense of mystery about the place – you can visualise monkeys and peacocks roaming around the garden with its lush ferns and palms enshrouding the house. This 'garden of ghosts' had even more surprising elements and creatures added to it when it was redesigned to include a swimming pool and lawn area.

This site is a large block of land, and not a typical Sydney residential property where the house overlooks the garden. The area for the pool is concealed beyond an arched cloister, retained from the former garden along with dabbed concrete and four-metre high brick boundary walls, palms, old stable doors, sandstone blocks and ladders. These various elements form the skeleton of the new 'pool room'.

Location *Sydney, Australia*
Project Team *Vladimir Sitta, Robert Faber*
Timeframe *2002*
Landscape Contractor *Above the Earth*

From the shady cloister, the area looks out into an elegant space with the pool reflecting the moods of the Sydney sky. While the garden appears deceptively simple, there is a lot more to it than meets the eye. The pool is along one side with no discernible fencing around it, a carport is on another side; there is also a grassy area with planting along the length of the pool and some decking ladders incorporated into a screen. New and found elements such as a monstrous fish skeleton in a tank form a 'quirky interpretation of the pool fence'. There is also a 1.2-metre high pool gate, an existing four-metre high boundary wall with a water spout concealed behind an old stable door, which actually leads nowhere, and alongside the pool a centuries-old device not often seen in suburban gardens, a ha-ha.

While this garden may have lost its former inhabitants, its latest transformation does not diminish the pervading atmosphere of the site's past. The designer feels that it persists 'in elements still present on the site'.

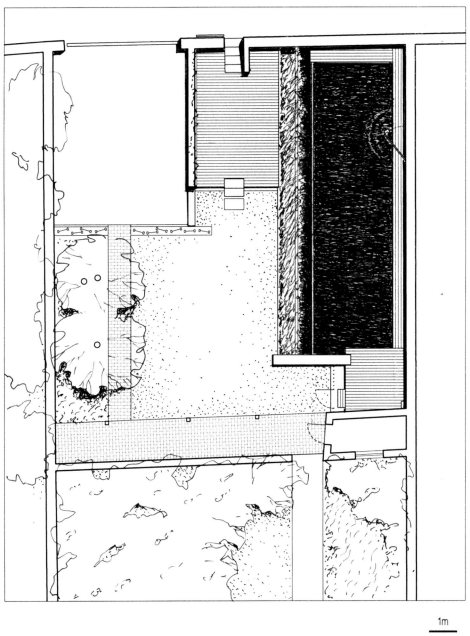

The spatial layout of the garden is deceptively simple

1m

G A R D E N   O F   G H O S T S

The new design elements are discreetly inserted into the former structure of the garden

Above left: The planted ha-ha alongside the pool

RED BLACK GARDEN

I f your homeland is ablaze with colour, it seems only natural to incorporate some of this into your new home. This site not only received a rich splash of colour but also a complete makeover from one of its new owners who was a migrant from Peru. Following the house renovations and addition of a deck, the upgrading of an awkwardly shaped 1970s swimming pool, surrounds and levels was undertaken prior to a redesign of the garden.

Several fundamental decisions guided the design of the garden. Level changes provided the key design concept and involved raising ground levels around the house, allowing direct access from house to garden, the addition of retaining walls to divide the garden into a pool space and upper terrace, new stairs, concealment of pool equipment and a screen to hide a neighbour's house.

Location *Sydney, Australia*
Project Team *Vladimir Sitta, Maren Parry*
Timeframe *2001*
Landscape Contractor *Above the Earth*

All these changes left little room for planting except on the perimeter. A pear tree was chosen for its compact form, but even this was too compact. The sculptural solution was to tie the lower branches with blue rocks to weigh them down and open them up. This Polynesian technique can be used to form unusual shapes and has added a further bright element to the dance of colour in this garden.

The client's Peruvian love of colour came to the fore both inside and outside the house once the alterations were complete. The pool was repaired and retiled in black, with bright red tiles laid in a random pattern forming the pool surrounds. A water channel with yellow glass mosaic tiles, partially covered with green pebbles, edges a wall. Finally a curving path was laid with reused bluestone.

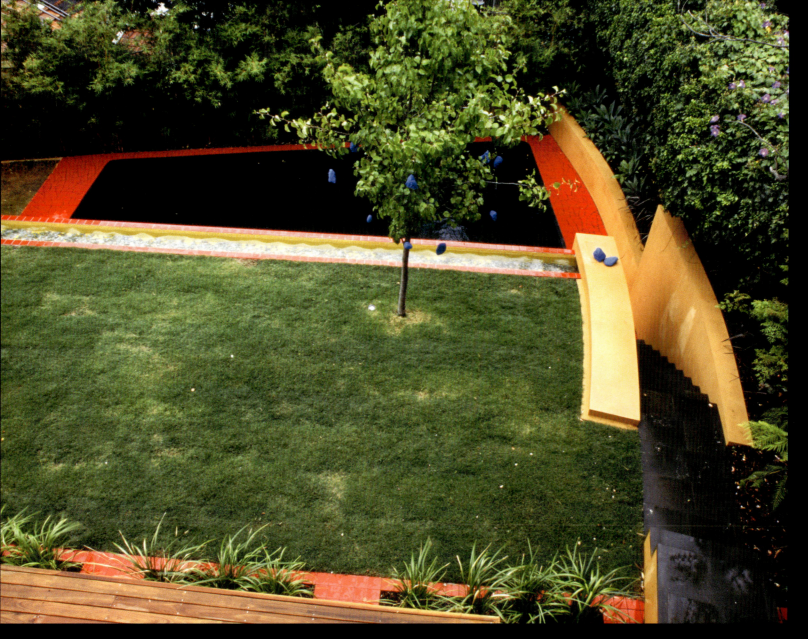

The restructured space and level changes transform the garden

The water channel with yellow glass mosaic tiles and pale green pebbles which accentuate level changes; Detail of decking and red tiling

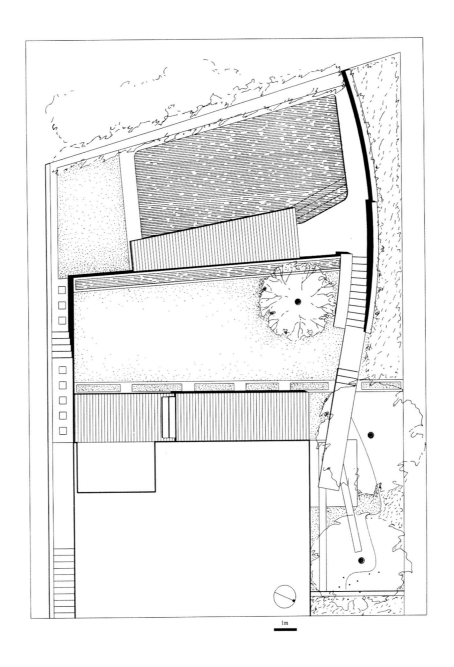

Plan showing how the house reconnects with the garden

RED BLACK GARDEN

BLURRING INSIDE AND OUT

Shimmering pool tiles slide down into the swimming pool and the colours melt into the depths. The chameleonesque skin of the pool is just one of the unexpected charms of this otherwise small back garden which offers all that a Sydneysider could desire.

Combining the briefs for both house and garden from the outset helped to reconcile the spatial challenge of incorporating a modest house extension and a swimming pool into the small space. The pool was built as an underlay to the building — 'the house cantilevers partially over the pool creating the illusion of a much larger water body,' explains Sitta. A deck spans the level change between house and garden and also serves as a barbecue area. The trees alongside the pool are lemon-scented eucalypts which replaced a protected tree damaged in a storm.

Location *Sydney, Australia*

Project Team *Vladimir Sitta, Robert Faber*

Timeframe *2003–2004*

Architect *Chris Elliott Architects*

Landscape Contractor *Landshapers*

Colour Consultants *D4*

Different forms and expressions of fences and gates
Previous page: By interlinking house and pool, there is space for everything

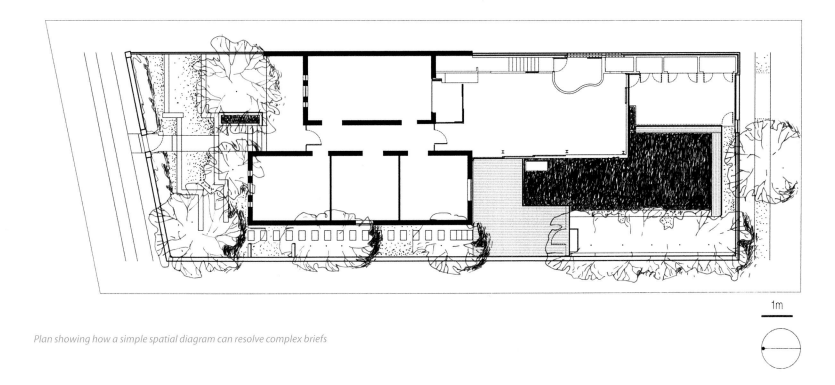

Plan showing how a simple spatial diagram can resolve complex briefs

1m

Where a safety fence was necessary, a quirky and different solution resulted. Vertical, stainless steel rods cross the narrowest section of the garden and pool and act as a safety rail between the shallow and deeper parts of the pool. Along the edge of the house an aquarium snuggles into a corner and an existing brick wall forms the last piece of the mandatory fence.

In the front garden, subtle changes included adding a water trough to edge the front steps and repositioning some sandstone flagging, which sits as comfortably in the garden as an old cat. The view of the house from the street, with its draping new hedge and enticing gate which is lit at night, belies the charms that await within.

117

BLURRING INSIDE AND OUT

difficult task to gain approval for the fenceless pool from local authorities but persistence won out. A fenceless pool is one of Sitta's foibles and one that he mostly achieves with the help of supportive clients. Concessions to council regulations resulted in a traditional gate and water retention requirements which are minor imposts compared with achieving this extraordinary effect of a sheet of blue against the bushland backdrop.

Location *Sydney, Australia*
Project Team *Vladimir Sitta*
Timeframe *1995–1996*
Architect *Catherine Sullivan Architects*
Landscape Contractor *Above the Earth*

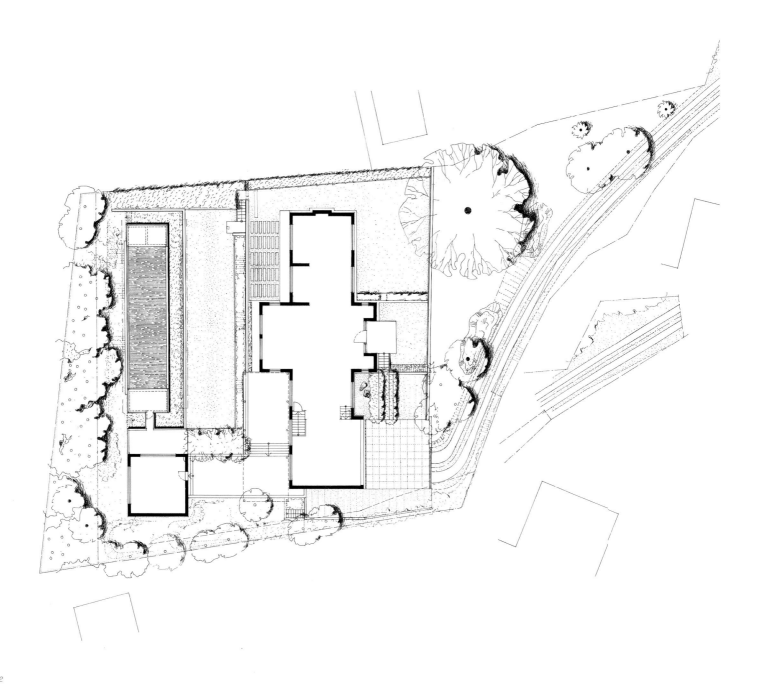

Plan of site
Opposite page: View of the lower terrace and swimming pool with planting of grasses in the moat alongside the pool

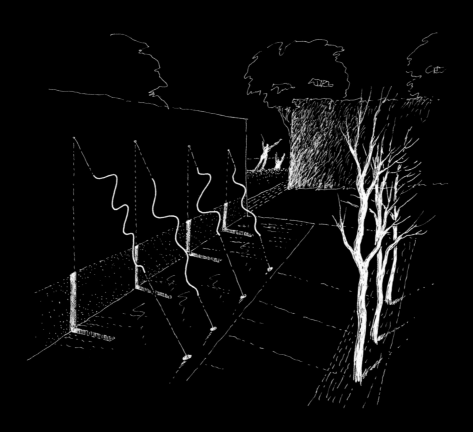

SUBURBAN ALCHEMY

THE RED GARDEN

For years, Sitta's 'doodles' were perceived as anomalies by many — impractical, theoretical drawings that were impossible to construct. That could well have been said about this garden after perusal of the initial sketches with their perilous planes of rock and cantilevered tree. For the design to be realised, it was vital that Sitta had a trusting and adventurous client and an architect with flair and pragmatism who believed in him. The raw materials for the design, combined with the unexpected, coalesced into this quite unlikely creation of a landscape reminiscent of the Australian interior. Sitta utilised sandstone found just beneath the site's ground level, a large collection of potted succulents and coincidently a sample of red desert stone left in his office whose properties intrigued him.

Location *Sydney, Australia*

Project Team *Vladimir Sitta, Maren Parry, Robert Faber*

Timeframe *2003– 2004*

Architect *Luigi Rosselli Architects*

Landscape Contractor *Bates Landscape Services*

The unexpected chemistry between the red stone and the plants inspired the composition of five angled planes concealing water pools. The garden evolved organically, with models used to develop the design. 'Originally my [Sitta's] intention was to let water ooze from stonework joints. However, water losses were too high, so we drilled through the wall and now have one discharge point only.' For designs with such irregular geometries as this one, there is a lot of site involvement, including on this occasion planting the client's succulents. They were placed quite consciously to both screen and borrow from the distant view of the harbour and to give the clients their 'illusion of a personal paradise'. In the foreground of the broader view is a swimming pool located along the short end of the garden. Here the colours of cooling greys, blues and greens echo the colours of the water.

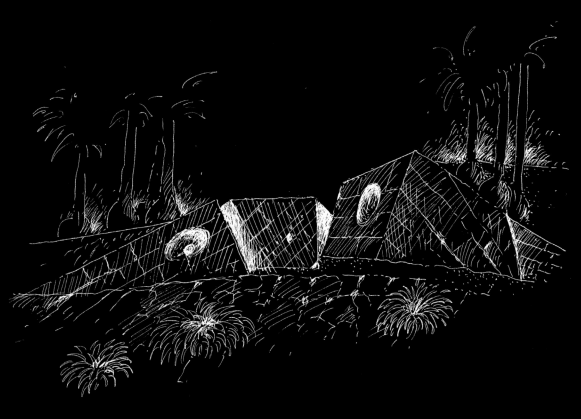

Doodles that shaped the garden
Opposite page: A pool is concealed under five angled rock ledges
Previous page: The irregular geometries of the thrusting rock ledges appear different from every angle

THE RED GARDEN

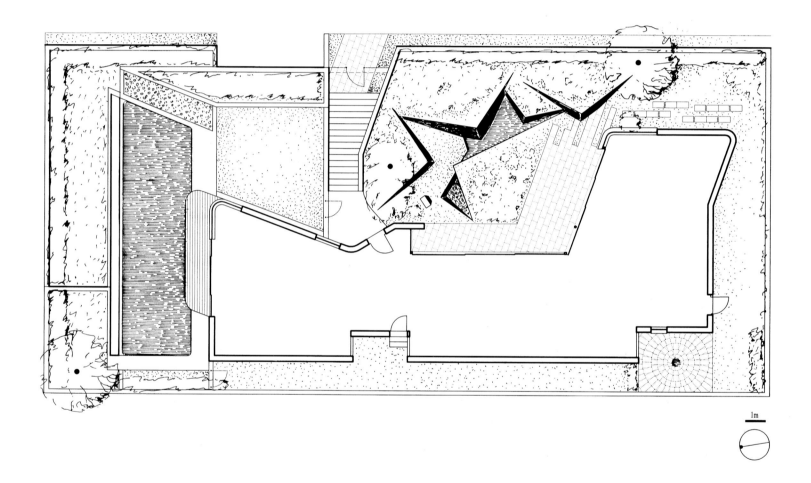

The plan shows how three-dimensional experiences can be captured in a suburban garden

Pools among the desert rocks contain unusual fish and a ceramic bird resides in one of the drill holes. A small court at the side of the house was intended to take the form of a receding cross, though due to problems with the size of the pieces of red slate (which are in fact purple in colour), Sitta was forced to use a spiral form circling down to a black hole, reminiscent of an Anish Kapoor or Goldsworthy sculpture. Unfortunately, after a kookaburra drowned there, the 'Black Hole' was planted out.

Note: The red sandstone was quarried near Alice Springs; the red slate used in the small courtyard also comes from the Northern Territory.

Red slate spiral

View of the swimming pool

THE GARDEN OF WALLS

O ften the most unlikely clients give the designer the greatest licence to create a personal paradise. This garden has arisen phoenix-like from a steeply sloping site with rocky sandstone outcrops. The design takes the innate abstractions, irregularities and relationships of the rock outcrops and massages them into a landscape fit for play — a ruined fortress collapsing into the landscape. Part of the clients' brief was to create a garden that was safe for their four children on a site with no large flat areas; the house extensions took most of the space occupied by the original garden. Designed as a series of friendly outdoor rooms, the new garden includes a Hills Hoist clothes line, a swimming pool, barbecue area and trampoline.

134

In the family's backyard, scattered toys confront the visitor. Burst water bombs, miniature furniture, plastic trikes, two cases of Fleur de Lys champagne and some extraordinary landscape architecture make up this exuberant chaos. What could have been a simple ascent via a few flights of steps has become an extravagant stage set for childhood adventures or an afternoon idyll. Up one flight of steps from the barbecue you find a child's trampoline, or up another is the Hills Hoist clothes line, and finally one last flight leads to the swimming pool. This ascent is hidden behind an artful composition of three principal landscape elements: natural sandstone outcrops; walls covered with fuchsia, orange and ochre coloured render; and plantings of *Pennisetum alopecuroides* and *Agave attenuata*.

Above and previous page: Views of the rendered walls and plantings of Pennisetum alopecuroides and Agave attenuata

The design team used a clay model to realise the non-Cartesian geometries of this landscape. Technical drawings were prepared taking measurements from the model. When construction began, the excavator revealed the exact extent of the sandstone outcrops beneath the soil. Rather than removal of the sandstone to make way for the construction, the unearthed outcrops were cleverly fused with the designed walls through careful on-site supervision. This increased the sculptural drama of the landscape while conveniently removing the need to construct foundations for the walls.

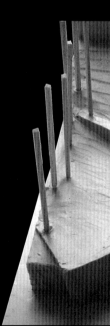

Construction involved excavation of existing sandstone and integration with retaining walls

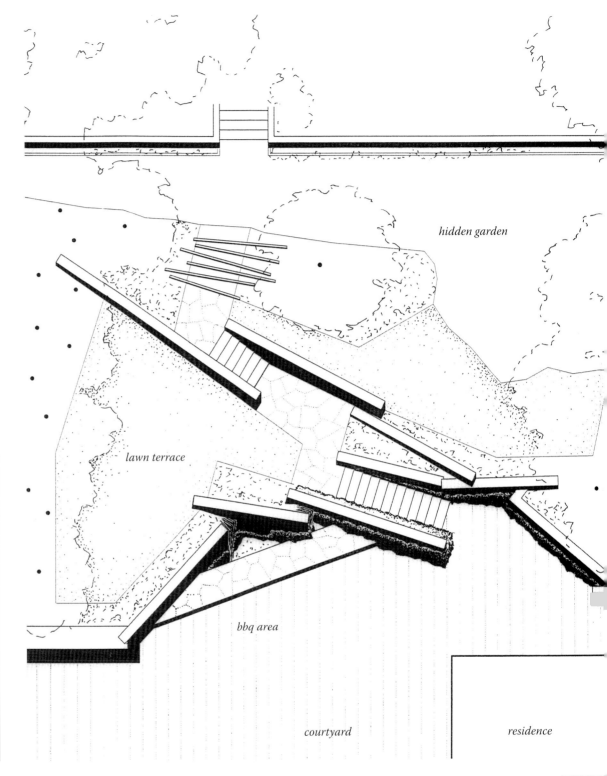

hidden garden

lawn terrace

bbq area

courtyard

residence

Plan of garden

Clay model of the garden

T H E   G A R D E N   O F   W A L L S

In this abstract landscape the decoration and patterning are left to the innate qualities and relationships of the materials used. The sandstone flagstones are covered by a filigree of lichens, the rocky outcrops ooze mossy water, the render develops a flowery patina, white pebbles move underfoot, sheltering crevices nurture unfurling ferns and walls grow fringes of succulents and grasses. Viewed from the patio the landscape becomes a colourful, textured scene reminiscent of a painting by Paul Klee. The bright walls do not become 'one' with the landscape, nor do they glide above it as a detached modernist expression. Instead the walls tackle the landscape on equal terms in a warped game of snakes and ladders; sliding, dipping, reaching. They sit upon the sandstone outcrops, jostling playfully rather than relinquishing their artificial origins.

The front of the house provides no hint of the surprise that awaits at the back. The designers have refused to be limited by the suburban aesthetic of the surrounding properties and have pursued their unique vision with the clients' support. The backyard functions as an escapist retreat by encompassing both the uncharted territory of a child's imagination and the directionless indolence of a summery barbecue.

The aesthetic of this garden may prove unsettling for some. This bold approach cannot be separated from an equally powerful invitation 'to play' — and the result is at once a confrontation and a temptation. By taking such risks, this garden awakens the senses; it is hard to begrudge the designers' wilfulness and so much easier to join in their childlike wonder at their creation. Paul Klee said that, when drawing, he liked 'to take a line for a walk'. Out of curiosity one must follow Klee's lines and end up dancing with space and colour. Such is the case with Vladimir Sitta's and Maren Parry's design for this garden.

* This garden description was co-authored by Scott Hawken.

Wedged between the rendered walls and existing sandstone are vertically piled pieces of slate

The rich render of the retaining walls provides a dramatic setting for the vegetation

GARDEN OF FIRE

At first glance, this doesn't look much like a garden except for a massive camphor laurel tree. A space such as this indicates how broad yet limiting the term 'garden' can be. For the clients, their property underwent a transformation from a small, dank, shady backyard into a poetic place with meaning that transcends its boundaries.

The clients' brief sought ways to enjoy their garden on a site with numerous constraints, including being overlooked by an unsightly apartment block. To deal with these problems, the space outside the semi-detached house was redefined in several ways. Firstly the camphor laurel tree with its richly textured bark was seen as a positive, compositional, vertical element. Alongside it a granite water channel now disappears into the background and beyond, thereby increasing the illusion of space. Rough-edged but precisely-cut low granite blades search out the edges.

Location *Sydney, Australia*
Project Team *Vladimir Sitta, Maren Parry*
Timeframe *1998*
Architect *Grose Bradley*

The fire ritual alight. The glow from the fire transforms the textured bark of the tree into an interesting design element

The rough-edged blades of granite

Outside the back doors of the house, rustling bamboo is suggestive of a larger plant-filled garden with leaves playing in the breeze and shifting light. The other main elements are a fire trail and a sculpture formed from a cruciform and golden egg. This sculpture has its own complex symbolism and imagery, which the client says is a 'wicked mixture of pagan belief and Christian structure. The whole, perhaps, Vladimir's metaphor for infinity and dabblings with metaphysics?'

The fire element in the garden defies notions about the sacrosanctity of property. Just as this garden is reminiscent of so many Lego pieces which can be gathered up and moved to another place, its design evokes a sense of the significant role that fire plays in the Australian landscape. Australian Aboriginals use fire as a technique for managing the landscape. As nomadic people, they leave few traces except for the burns from their fires and this aspect of their culture is exemplified in the ritualistic fire trail created by Sitta.

The fire trail

The ephemeral elements of this garden challenge any ideas about permanence — they will take time to establish and mature before they can be fully appreciated. This site may lack the physical planting structure of a formal garden but the joy of it is that the owners can pack it up and take it with them to their next destination.

Further reading: Barbara Rook, 'Convergences — A Vladimir Sitta Garden', *Landscape Australia*, no. 3, 1999: 200–201.

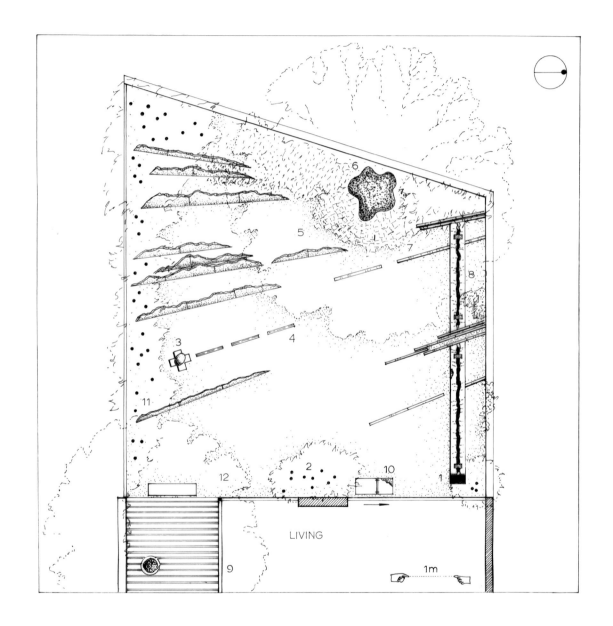

LIVING

1m

The plan shows how a few elements can transform every dimension and storyline of a space

G A R D E N   O F   F I R E

This homestead, just outside Canberra, has all of the comfortable qualities one would expect of an established working rural property. Around the house, extensive manicured lawns, walks among spreading trees, thick hedges that shield the house from the elements, a vegetable garden and a pool inevitably lead to the endless dry, rough grass and tall skeletal trees beyond. Concealed behind Himalayan cypress hedges is a garden as large as a Royal Park and designed from 'a series of suggestive fragments and visual metaphors that are brought together only by those who elect to explore them,' Sitta explains.

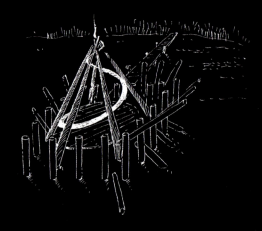

Location *South Western Slopes, NSW, Australia*
Project Team *Vladimir Sitta*
Timeframe *1989–ongoing*
Architect *Ian Little*
Landscape Contractor *Carl Valerius (Stage 1) and Dan & Dan (Stage 2)*

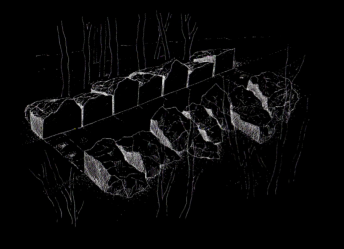

The European clients had a pragmatic brief for Sitta. They wanted the garden to be an extension of the living spaces, to act as a screen and include water elements that could be viewed from indoors. They also wanted a tennis court and swimming pool and, a bonus for the designer, they 'were adventurous enough to virtually give me a blank page,' Sitta says. While there was an existing garden, there was little for him to work with.

Above from top: Detail sketch of the garden; The formal lawn

The water element of the brief provided the key to this garden and its new layout. The hot summers in this part of Australia are merciless and water and shade are essential to survive them. Water takes on different forms and is dispersed throughout the garden rooms, which were built incrementally, yet appear to unfold naturally from one to the next. These often draw their character and inspiration from an artifact or historical detail retained from the old garden.

GARANGULA

Some of the garden rooms express how inventive and humorous a garden can be. Take, for example, the outdoor spa — when relaxing in the split stone conical enclosure on a hot day, you can look either up to a writhing roof of twisted copper rods or across to a sinuous etched fissure cut through the edge of the pool. 'It's a joke,' Sitta explains. 'This property used to be called Black River Farm, but there was no river, so we made one.' Alternatively, you can press a button any time and the space will be immersed in a fog of water vapour which transforms the pool into an ephemeral river.

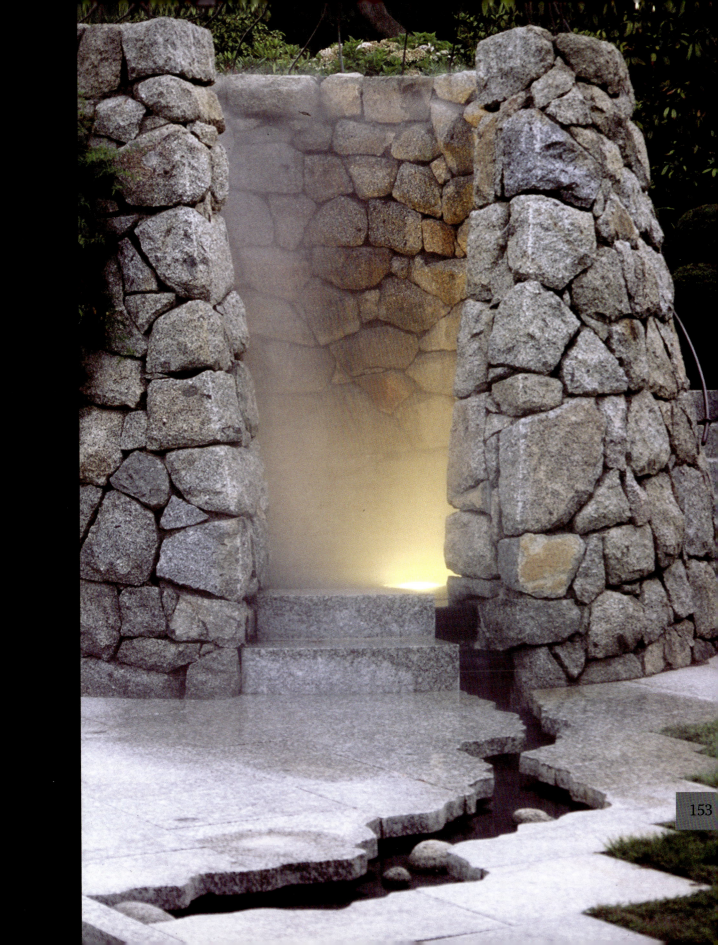

A crater garden forms another cooling enclosure, with stairs enticing you down into a sunken area. Encircling this area is a 'cathedral' of Italian alders trained to bend forward and form a canopy over the cavity.

Expansive palatial lawns with sculptures and parterre gardens stretch out towards the vista of rolling hills beyond the hedges, rides and forests. The hint of much more to discover exists beyond the surrounding hedges.

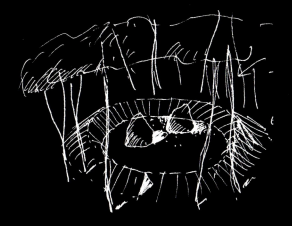

Above and left: The tree cathedral – a circle of Italian alders

155

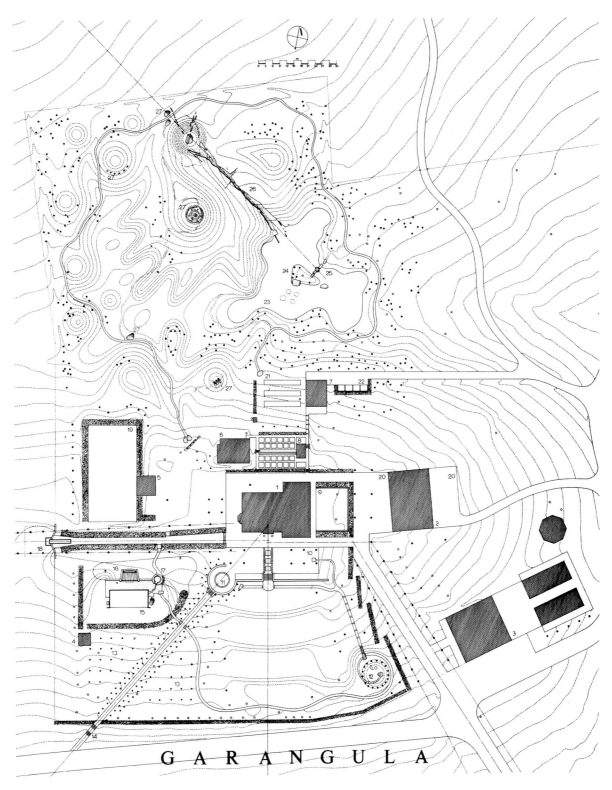

Plan of garden
Opposite page: The sculpture lawn

GARANGULA

CHAUMONT SUR LOIRE

The competition entry for the 1995 Chateau Chaumont sur Loire Festival of Parks and Gardens highlights the metaphysical aspect of Sitta's doodles, which rarely find expression in domestic gardens. The theme of the festival was 'Curiosity Gardens' and Sitta's response was 'Nihilium', whose form is focused on an arched timber wall and a compilation of other disparate elements and juxtapositions which are described as creating 'precarious balances and dubious relationships which subjugate the viewer'.

The piece is full of modernist contradictions, dichotomies and ambiguities that weave extremes together on either side of the wall. There are so many stories and ideas contained here that it almost defies description as a second-hand experience. Even so, it is a provocative design, one that could set your teeth on edge.

Location *Chaumont sur Loire, France*

Project Team *Vladimir Sitta*

Timeframe *1995*

Landscape Contractor: *Conservatoire International des Parcs et Jardins et du Paysage*

162

Certainly a 'curious' garden, 'Nihilium' raises more questions than answers. Some of these persist beyond the life of the piece and are typical of Sitta's design technique, namely 'What was living and what was dead? What was visible and what was invisible?' (commentary from the competition catalogue). This last question can be asked of many of Sitta's domestic garden designs: the viewer is often enticed with tantalising allusions and experiences, only to find that the garden is actually comprised of quite ephemeral elements and minimal physical structure.

From left: The main bower structure with plants discharging into empty pots; Other extrusions from the bower wall

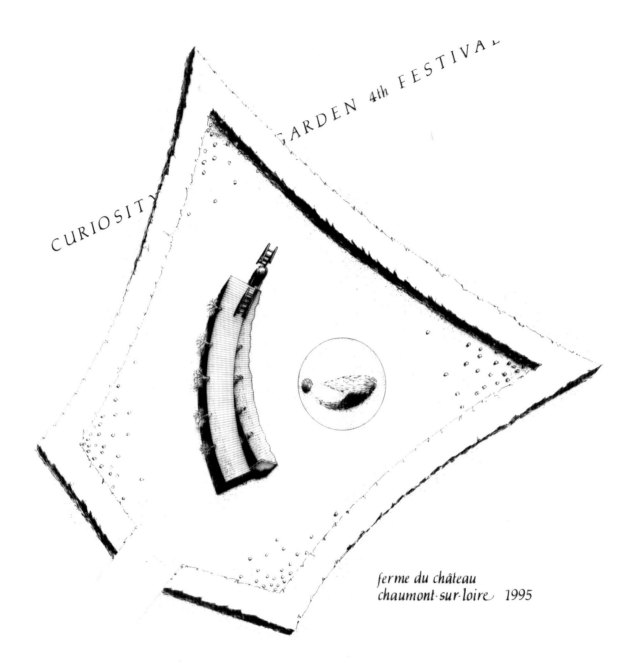

CURIOSITY GARDEN 4th FESTIVAL

ferme du château
chaumont·sur·loire 1995

At one end of the 'Nihilium' garden is a ladder broken by a conifer covered in duck feathers appearing to pass through the wall, while the other end of the wall is blackened with bitumen. Living and inert elements, which are either beautiful or repulsive (aesthetically or by connotation), are juxtaposed and inserted into the metre-thick wall structure. These include bones, red poppies for their allusion to blood, tortured trees, wounds, the eerie ticking of a metronome, peepholes containing small perspex containers with various specimens such as giant cockroaches and deadly insects warped by the plastic, and even US dollar bills.

163

FURTHER READING

Bradley-Hole, C. (2005), *The Minimalist Garden*. Mitchell Beazley, London.

Harpur, J. (2007), *Gardens in Perspective: Garden Design in Our Time*. Mitchell Beazley, London.

Hobhouse, P. (2006), *Great Gardens of the World: In Search of Paradise*. Frances Lincoln, London.

Jones, L. (2003), *Reinventing the Garden: Chaumont — Global Inspirations from the Loire*. Thames & Hudson, London.

Richardson, T. (2008), *Avant Gardeners*. Thames & Hudson, London.

Weller, R. (2005), *Room 4.1.3: Innovations in Landscape Architecture*. University of Pennsylvania Press, Pennsylvania.

Wilson, A. (2002), *Influential Gardeners: Shaping Today's Style*. Mitchell Beazley, London.